PSYCHOLOGICAL
SKULLDUGGERY

*"In a world of manipulation,
deceit, and ruthlessness, is of the
norm and all is fair play."*

P.Los

authorHOUSE®

AuthorHouse™
1663 Liberty Drive
Bloomington, IN 47403
www.authorhouse.com
Phone: 1-800-839-8640

First published by AuthorHouse 5/10/2010

ISBN: 978-1-4520-1062-5 (e)
ISBN: 978-1-4520-1061-8 (sc)

Printed in the United States of America
Bloomington, Indiana

This book is printed on acid-free paper.

CONTENTS

INTRODUCTION

What a world we live in today! Many of us never thought that this beautiful world we live in, would ever be so treacherous by leaders, politicians, teachers, ministers, and everyday people. Those of us that have love ones do all we can to protect them from this heartless cold topsy-turvy world. Child-molesters are getting released from jails and prisons daily, only to go out and apply their inhumane craft of abducting under-age girls and boys for their sick pleasures. Some sadistic murderers are killing trying to make a name for themselves, and some murderers are paid to kill or murder another human-being because that's their means of survival. They're call contract killers. Many of us have asked ourselves, how can another human- being murder or kill another human with no remorse. To murder, kill, molest, rape, manipulate, lie, cheat and defraud someone else, comes with a certain psychology. Whether that frame of mind is debauched, influenced by drugs or alcohol, suffering from a terrible past experience of some sort, or an extreme reason to change with the times to survive, and whatever may be the reason why some people make extreme changes one thing for sure, it exist. Only a damn fool will believe other-wise.

There are numerous reasons why I chose to write this book concerning the minds of society. Like ruthless politicians and business owners, what's happening on a daily bases, how to use this type of mind to achieve your goal, also recognize when psychological skullduggery is being used on you. Another reason why I felt it was imperative to write this book, is because I'm a parent and I have love ones. My back-ground and past life has taught me, by living on the streets, entering the business world, working with psychiatrist and psychologist for ten years plus, and also working, and associating with lawyers, prominent business people, and being a Fellow-Brethren of the Auasrian Mystery Order and the B.Y.E. Brotherhood; that life is a constant battle ground and warfare. You either fight to win, opting-out, or not knowing; which leads to your own demise. It takes a certain type of mind or pyshology to survive in this heartless world. As we go futher into this book; I will show you why you should have the psychology of the fox, adaptability like a chameleon, and the heart of a bull to survive or reach your goal. You must understand the world you're living in at this present time. I'm not writing to promote or glorify this art called skullduggery; I'm writing so that you may see and maybe understand by all means about this psychology that has no restraints and remorse when it's used. Many writers have written on this topic, without the actual experience of facing death or any type of perilous bodily encounter head on, where the mind automatically does what it's trained to do without thinking. Most of these writers use common logic without practical reasoning, and never has been in the situation that they're writing about. To speak on something without experience and not having actual insight of knowing is a total idiot. Basically, the writer is appealing to your naivety, which can give you a mental burst at the time without the proper psychological training. If you were to take any of these writers, who wrote on the subject of war strategies, and survival on these mean streets of America. I know for surety over half of them couldn't psychologically handle some of these war zones here in America, and try to apply that scholastic training in the core of these inner cities or even sign up in the military to fight for their country which they say the love so much. It's all hype and gibberish! Many would probably say, "Who would go to the ghetto, inner city, a war zone just to prove a point; that they can survive in an area, where murdering, drug-dealing, drive-by shooting, con men, scamers and damners apply their craft and trade every single day of their lives?" Me, I have been there, on the streets of down-trotting territories, with the homeless, drug-abusers, alcoholics, the street bullies, ex-cons, or psychotic maniacs, the drug-dealers, con-men, players of women, which I myself was a "womanizer" or "playboy" as some called us players in the game of controlling women for that American dream, the green, the money!! So, having a psychological mind of skullduggery, was my means of survival on a daily bases. Without skullduggery you couldn't surive on the streets. You either was the victim of the con-men games, pimps persuasion, mack-men smooth debonair, players using great verbatim in seducing you to believe and see things their way. When you were under their spell, you might have gotten taking for a certain amount of money, jewelry, or performing some type of act and you were the pawn. When these street hustlers, molesters, and psychological skullduggery minded people, get busted and get thrown in jail or prison for their crimes, inside the jails and prisons they just hone the skills, and when they come out with that rehabilitated psychological skullduggery, society has a great monopoly on its hands. Because there's no, no street codes and rules anymore, its dog eat dog, fuck me and I'll fuck you, do me and I'll do you, and if need be I'll do you anyway is the motto of the human psychological make-up. Whether political, business, religion, and world-wide, politicians are supposed to work and serve the people, but now they manipulate and deceive the people who pay taxes, which is a source of their income. Without their personal investments, and they're destroying the people means to survive, which is their God given human right; to run the course of life till there's no more, but these psychological skullduggery heartless manipulators are destroying life and this Universe as we know it. Corporate warfare is very prevalent among business and politicking. Control is the norm and tone of life at the present time. CEOs' are receiving millions of dollar bonuses that they know will cause the business to flop and go bankrupt, and leave these hard-working parents with children in the cold, with no means of income to survive. Ministers are owning mansions, having conglomerate of women, businesses, cars, and millions of other peoples' money. When ministers have no greater spiritual knowledge than those who are giving their hard earned dollars.

So, I conclude with this introduction, that if anyone wants to be ahead of the game of life, or enrich their life, obtain power, control people to make them your own personal pawns, here's the know how. If you don't know how, you never will achieve that so-called American Dream. It's easy to tell a lie, but great manipulators don't lie, they just alter the situation or the story they're telling to seduce you emotionally if you're a woman, and use reverse psychology on your mind, if you're a man without you noticing what just happened. We'll get to that later in the book, concerning the mental and emotional effects skullduggery can have on anyone. I say again dear reader, it takes a certain type of mind, a certain type of person to apply this psychological skullduggery tactics, and awareness that's needed on a daily bases. Whether it's business, politics, relationships, and in society where it's mostly needed. I'm not speaking on what ought to be or what can be I'm emphasizing on what is!!

IMPERATIVE OR PERILOUS

Let us explore to see why it is imperative or perilous, to use psychology skullduggery in our times like it has been greatly implemented in past times. This imperative art called skullduggery has been used by people we would least expect to use a form of its tactic or strategy, whether it's a child that's being manipulative to get its way, CEOs' and administrators at your job holding the monthly meeting, your minister in his or her camouflaged velvet suit, with a iron heart and a open hand. Maybe it's your husband, boyfriend, girlfriend, wife, the police officer, the teacher, politicians, society or that imperative or perilous means within you? Many of us have been told that our own minds, is our own worst damn enemy! If that's so, how did we get this enemy within us? Did it just appear there out of no where or was it constant mind conditioning from our parents, teachers, ministers or is it the daily propaganda we're exposed to. We must first know where and how this so-called enemy skullduggery arrived. Before anything devastating with an enormous potential threat is lurking to do great harm from afar or within our boundaries can be destroyed, it has to be acknowledged that it's real. The person with keen prudence can see threats and deception before they're implemented, whether someone is trying to gain financially, manipulate the person to be their loyal pawn, or using the person to be their scapegoat. One of the main reasons people are being taking by hook or crook, is people have a problem with listening. They've mistaken the ears for listening, when the ears have nothing to do with listening. The ears are strictly for sound and sound only!! Listening is a mind mechanism. Paying close attention to what the person is saying, whether physical, verbal or what they're not say verbally, and what their eyes are doing is a must. Sometimes you have to be aware of what they're not saying, while they're talking and rattling on to set you up for the kill. Many have written on this, but what they don't tell you is this. If your mind is being occupied with its own thoughts, you are definitely not listening to the other person. Sometimes it's good to let the other person see and think you're not paying attention, when in actual and factual you're definitely zeroed in on their tactics. When you're not giving attention to the deceiver, which is what they need to deceive you, they can't. But in order to do this you have to listen, observe them carefully to see what they're saying and doing. Now, stealing is a different thing that's not deception, that's thievery a lower scale act or performance. But for some it works or helps, but big gains and big pay-offs come from psychological skullduggery. Because over time the person is being brain-washed and can't see the enemy's strategy shaping and molding their minds, that have been planted by a master manipulator. So, this master of skullduggery is controlling your thoughts and behaviors, without you even realizing it, because you've created an unseen habit. We all know that habits are hard to kick, and there's no treatment for habits that appeal to your happiness and self gratification. So, this master, that uses skullduggery over a long periods of time is getting the best of you in a worst way. How can you confront or acknowledge the enemy that you basically have created? You can't confront or acknowledge anything that you can't see or know that it exist. It takes someone else to inform you, that has the prudence to recognize it. Here's where the problem comes in. When we're being confronted about our behaviors, we either get defensive or offensive and sometimes both. The only one that's getting the joy of it all, is the person who has a great understanding on the imperatives and perilous use of psychological skullduggery for their benefit. The longer this mental brain-washing goes unchecked the more beneficial you become for that someone else; who's a great puppeteer, that's pulling your strings. As long as these tactics of psychological skullduggery is being utilized on you emotionally and mentally, you'll forever be entrapped by your own devices. That's why our own minds, are our own great downfall, but someone else's immensely great gain. Not only is this the reason timid minds are so prevalent, not only can the timid be someone else's puppet, they can also be the cause of them doing harm to the innocent or running off a love one. So, our greatest ally we can count on, is our own mind's potential to excel for greatness. This comes from mastering self and then others, instead we're being controlled by the real internal conflicting enemy, ourselves, and the lack of our shrewdness to understand. This unchecked art of skullduggery, that has performed this mental implementation within us can lead to an alcoholic, a drug-abuser, a molester, spouse cheater and beater, lazy-blamer, a great hindrance on society's progress, an immense threat and harm to many human-beings at large, it all depends on the person that's implementing this art. Another thing that is imperative with skullduggery, is learning to quiet the mind. A mind at peace is a mind that's never disturbed by others or bombarded with many unconstructive thoughts that attacks the mind with great fury. This tactic is used by martial-artists to maneuver their opponents, and not to show fear in the face of harm. Whenever you're unable to control your thoughts, you are able to be manipulated by others that do have the potential to control their mind. So, basically, their thoughts become your thoughts. It's like putting your brain inside their skull. Now, you have a human robot. The mind has nothing to do with emotion, it can only acknowledge emotions or feelings. That's why performing psychological skullduggery is only for the elected few. You have to know when to use your emotions and not let your emotions move you. Using psychological skullduggery is how great men and women achieved their greatness in life. Using mind over emotions, and understanding that emotions is only fuel and intense passion to carry them through the necessary defeats and turmoil before their goal is reached. So, before psychological skullduggery can be implemented by anyone, you have to understand the mind, know the goal you're aiming for, and also know what's perilous. If you get caught trying to apply this craft without the know how; the only achievement you will achieve is many defeats and severe set-backs. Deception and lies are similar, but different in scope and tactics. If you don't know how to deceive, you can't get away with a beautiful lie. The art of knowing how to deceive comes with certain body gestures, certain speech tone and volume, and rhetoric with theatrical movements. You also need to know what are the other person's emotional ties and weaknesses. Knowing what makes the other person become defensive or offensive, gives you the upper hand to apply skullduggery without stalemate. Another device of skullduggery, is an imperative form of propaganda that comes from television, radio, magazines and etc,. The people we associate with can be manipulative and influence us much easier than a stranger, and the psychological skullduggery puppeteers that who corporate this club. Those who manipulate the laws, politicians, businesses, financial banking systems, education, and certain men and women in society all perform this art with great strategy. When the puppeteers manipulate the politicians, then we in society become the victim of their control, power, and wealth. Then it becomes a great dividing line between the super-rich and the very extreme poor people. Next, the victims, which are the poor people become thieves, killers, and terrorize society like Godzilla, but in human form with monstrous catastrophic acts. These criminals become inmates at the same time the politicians and puppeteers get the monies from these same people that were manipulated to commit these crimes. Then, the tax-payers are forced to pay more taxes, to house and feed these criminals. So, taxes are forced to get raised enormously, which becomes more money for the manipulators. So, in essence politicians see the imperative art and gain of skullduggery. If you ever notice whenever a former president, congressman, politician, war general retires from their formal post of work or office, you always get to see the lies, deception, and skullduggery performed by them when they were in office. We're the ones who pay the price behind these lies. Because we believe what they're telling us is truthful, their strategies had to be carried out for the nation's benefit. They also inform us what they should do or what they're forced to do, when in actuality, we're being deceived, and played on because of our lack of prudence to see behind the enemy's mask and rhetoric. This is psychological skullduggery at it's best. So, learning to listen carefully to words and bodily gestures is acknowledging how, when, where, and who is getting set you up for tactical psychological skullduggery to be used on you. Finally, we should all pay close attention to our random thoughts that effect us negatively. There's a great benefit that comes with a mind of awareness, and knowing the benefits of utilizing this great art of psychological skullduggery. This art has been used by many prominent people of history, mainly politicians, war generals, religious leaders, billionaires, millionaires, martial artists, business tycoons, interrogators, pimps, players, mack-men, and con-men. Only the masters of this art, know if this art is applied with prudence and accuracy will their goal be accomplish. This prudence and accuracy has kept rulers of empires in power for centuries. The imperative and perilous tactics and strategies of psychological skullduggery can become a plaguing oppositional force, whenever it's being used without the proper procedures to manipulate for a big gain, big pay-off, and control. It can be very dangerous, when the victim or that sleeping giant awakes. So, the main thing is to keep your victims sleep as long as you can, to obtain all that's worth having. Persuading a person can be quite easy. The difficulty is keeping them persuaded over long periods of time. Only a master of this art can keep their victim persuaded over time, because the master knows, that with time all things mental, physical, spiritual, and socially will change, which will affect the person's disposition . Those that fail to change when time presents an opportunity to change will fail. When the course of time demands a change and the person doesn't change only brings their on down-fall. The wise and masters of psychological skullduggery understand change and its importance.

Those that do and Those that don't

Do you have what it takes to carve out your destiny at all cost? Are you willing to knave, manipulate, and deceive to reach the top which is the pedestal of successful leaders, dictators, and business tycoons? Is being mediocre satisfying and agreeable with you? If so, welcome to the world where exploitation is for those who know what it takes to reach the top and become very successful. Many people have written books, delivered sermons, and held seminars that honesty is better, when the majority of people lie everyday to themselves, with excuses and fears. We all would agree that it is morally right to be honest with one another. Being honest today is very costly, when you don't have that keen insight to see people for who they really are. Today many of us are using our eyes more than we use our minds and ears. Looking at things externally most of the time, one will never see the core of what their looking at. Not many people are willing to go to great lengths to see the reality of a situation, which is hard evidence and truth. Many will assume and make opinionated guesses, and base their lives on unproven theories. It's better to do something and error, than do nothing an assume what can and could be. This is the mentality and character of cowards and mediocre people. These cowards are people who masters of skullduggery know they're easy and ready for the picking. There's one thing I must make mention when dealing with cowards. They're not equipped for strenuous and perilous demanding endeavors, unless they have the backing of someone brave at their side. Which can be a downfall, when you have to wind up doing the majority of the work. This only means you're no longer in power, you're a tool for those that have power, or those that are striving to obtain a power post. Using skullduggery is mainly to keep you out, the lime-light of exposure, which can lead to you having despisers and haters that are willing to bring your demise at all cost. It's much more powerful to pull the strings and let the puppet take the stage, which is addictive to many to look as though there're successful, when in reality you're reaping the profits. Those who know that other peoples' money and time is how to get rich and richer; are those who will obtain power and become more powerful over time. The more money and power you obtain means you're taking more from people at an alarming rate, which only ensures you of your successful means of knowing how to perform skullduggery like many before you have. The powerful only have allies that are important to their goals and achievements. When you're powerful, it's easy to manipulate those on a lower rank, that's desperate for a mentor with great status. When those on a lower rank have the opportunity to rub elbows with the successful, they're willing to do everything to prove they have what it takes to be successful, and powerful like their mentors and leaders. This gives the mentor all the time and room to perform skullduggery with ease. There's nothing more glorious than to have a willing pawn. Those that know what it takes to reach the top are resilient, determined, and willing to charm those that need to be charmed for the opportunity to rise to great heights. Those that don't use these tactics to carve out their destiny, or become powerful will always be moved like pawns on the chessboard of life for the wealthy and powerful kings, queens, prince, princesses, rulers, and leaders throughout their entire lives. Life is a relationship where give and take are the daily norm. The powerful gives or rewards their subordinates with meager gifts, whether it's an additional small amount of money, jewelry, a trip or etc,. This is only for the subordinates to be loyal pawns to their mentors. Powerful leaders remain in power by using the art of psychological skullduggery to play on the hearts and capture the minds of their subordinates. Those that are willing to be truthful at all times, will sooner or later see that truth has no place or room where those that are powerful, and perform schemes on the weak. Those that are striving to reach the top understand that this journey of success is like shit to a farmer's boot, and dirt to a gardener's hands. Many have tried to climb this ladder with great stride only to be labeled reckless and foolish, by the mediocre people that are too timid to make their life what they want it to be at all cost. Skullduggery is also performed by banks, when the mediocre or less fortunate people are in need of a loan. The bank-teller will call the financiers, and the financier will call the higher-ups, which will follow the protocol set by the owner or owners. To give the money only at a higher rate, which is to have the borrower in their pockets over a long period of time and to get back thrice as much than was gave. So, in essence, the mediocre is only giving those that are powerful more power, wealth, and influence to make more demands on their daily lives. When you utilize this art of skullduggery it places people in a situation where they need you. That means you have a choice either to smother(suppress) or soothe them, to your own liking and needs. Those that are willing to take will always have power and wealth. Those that take with greed and larceny from those that don't, will leave those that don't with little means of substance to fiend for the lives. In due time they will not be at your mercy, because you have taken away their means and need for their survival. This only means you have lost leverage to remain in power, which will bring your condemnation by those that see their leader perform acts of greed, and not the art of psychological skullduggery. However, they will be seen and labeled as psychotic tyrannical acts. Many of them will have group discussions with their associates, hold rallies to demeanor those that take away their freedom of needs and wants. They will influence the people that it's wrong and its procedure will be thought of as the devil's advocate. When the people start a rebellion it's an indication that your tactics of skullduggery have been identified as greed. There have been people in our time and history that were unjust and greedy whether they were dictators, leaders, war generals, business tycoons, monarchs, or powerful people that misused this art, because of one major slip. Many fail to see that humans haven't changed much from past times to the present, which mean the hearts of men and women are still fickle, selfish, and lascivious when it suits their own personal gains and means of happiness. Those that are willing to remain in power will have to resort to nefarious means under the guise of appearing humane. Using skullduggery you have to appear to be fair and honest from the start, which can reward you with much room to apply your trade of skullduggery, and get all that's worth getting as fast you can, and how you to build a strong powerful fortress from those unwanted mercenary minded people. Those who obtain their power, wealth, and reach their goal have more reasons to always be prudent and see unwanted attacks from afar. The most influential and powerful will have a few within their boundaries or circle, that are willing to be loyal, intelligent, and prudent for their leader or mentor to remain in power, which has a great deal to do with their status, wealth and lifestyle. Those that are willing to do what's necessary to reach the top and obtain power, status, wealth, and influence will always be highly praised and admired by those that wish to, but are too timid to carry out the act. "Remember, I'm writing about the way things are, and not how they should be!!"

CAPITALIZES AND REALIZES

Those that know that in order to capitalize and carve out their dreams must invest in their mind, time, and energy. Whoever realizes that in order to achieve wealth and power, one must capitalize off other people's needs and wants. Basically, you have to create a means to serve the people, to purchase things that you provide. Realizing what people want and need is the first step to achieving your means of capitalizing. Now, without capital to start the business, and moving up the ladder of success, one will realize that what you need is half the battle. The main thing is knowing what's needed, what means you have to go about getting it, obtaining money to invest, and capitalize by all means for your present stability and golden years. To obtain status and power in the present times, has much to do with advertising and a great deal of psychological propaganda. Many business tycoons and politicians have emerging business investments, which strategically control the laws of operating a day to day business. This day to day system controls the employment for the people, and controls their progress of their investments and the progress for their co-investors. Capitalist that utilize skullduggery understand that deceit or trickery, is used to gain status, power, money, and not to strip the people of their liberty of purchasing power, but ensure the capitalist of more capital and unconquerable power to strive economically through inflation, deflation, and economical collapses. This is the back-bone of this American economical system. The big- business tycoons know that in order to control the money you control the markets, and you control the cash-flow. The people will always be effected in some form or fashion, when it comes to their life-line, which should give an indication to the leaders or would-be leaders of their tactics and strategies. The capitalist should always make the people feel as though their input is considered, when in reality it's never considered but appear to be. This reinforces their means of reigning longer by the people. Any person that plans to rule or control must at all cost, be prudent enough to hear and see what the public demands or request in order to appear civil and liberal. Now, over time it can become a nuisance to the leaders or capitalists to always be at the request of the people. That's when the leaders' loyal advisors is mostly needed to assist in maintaining the equilibrium between the people, the ruler or capitalist. Many large businesses encourage their employees to enroll in colleges and universities, which is a two-fold encounter, that most people fail to understand and consider why! One reason is when you apply for loans, you are basically putting money back in the capitalist pockets, which is other people's money from the start. That is being given on promissory note with great interest-rates. Now, the borrower is forced to use his or her time and knowledge of their schooling to pay-back the loan. So, now the one that received the loan is the worker, which empowers the capitalist to continue to grow more powerful and richer over time. Another thing that CEOs take in consideration, is that it forces them to pay more money to the employee if the person or persons that are hired considering their degree status and the salary that has to be paid for the position. Sometimes this can be a great asset to the business, if the person has loyalty, qualification and the mental capacity for the position that needs to be filled. That's when capitalist have to realize to see what is what, in order to stay afloat. In order to capitalize off other people, there are many important things to consider psychologically, strategically, and informally. Psychologically you have to weigh your options, strategically you have to consider what ground plans that need to be utilized. Finally gather all the information from day to day operations of the business, and be cognitive of the peoples' needs, wants, and emotional content. Without this vital information, no one can perform skullduggery without knowing what makes and breaks that person or persons. Only those that realize, what is takes to capitalize, why they're ambitious and resilient to capitalize, and what's at stake to achieve greatly and capitalize is the only way they can be a powerful playing skullduggery capitalist. Lets also mention that millions of stimulus dollars these businesses and banks are receiving, will only benefit themselves and not the businesses. These stimulus packages or monies that these CEOs are receiving will not help the economy, when employment is declining at an alarming rate. So, here the same practices and habits that caused major companies to file bankruptcy and also cause major lay-offs to be repeated is very staggering. So, in essence banks are unable to lend money, when employment is on the decline, for people to receive any type of loans and payback these loans for businesses to prosper. Anyone that has been a CEO,COO, and CFO for over fifteen or twenty years know the upside and down-side of businesses, economical market strategies, and know what's needed for global prosperity. The public is being told everything except what's truthful and real concerning the world economy and employment. All these big capitalists at the top of these businesses, political investors, and the wealthy secret elite circle know the plans and schemes they're implementing, which is psychological skullduggery with aggressive propoganda and mental manipulation to shield the reality of these plans for power, control, and economical domination.

Mind verses Emotion

Here's the constant battle or paradoxes of life. In other words, the warfare between mind and emotion. Many of us have great deals of seeing, but fail to know what's real and what's an illusion. Manipulators, con-men, and anyone who plays on the hearts and minds of individuals know, that in order for the trickery to work smoothly 95% of the time, the strategy, and tactics has to be undetected in order to effect the person emotionally. Majority of people today and in past times were moved and guided by their emotions. Now, there's a great deal of difference between our gut feelings, than just being emotionally concerned with some incident or occurrence. Our gut feelings, which are our basic instinct will tug away at us greatly over periods of time until the emotion or feeling is revealed. The paradox of feeling and thinking can lead to a major break-down, which can put you in a vulnerable position. When this happens the vulnerable person becomes an easy prey for the predator to move in and take advantage with ease. If, the predator is a person with acute foresight and cleverness, the predator will become important to the person that's being manipulated. Because the emotional ties have been created it appears to be a necessity, to always want to be with that person at all cost. This is a form of psychological skullduggery, where the mind has the upper-hand over emotion. Too much emotion can and will always blind the person's capacity to think rational and logically see what is going on around them. A person without a rational mind will be a person that acts strictly on emotion. Over time these unchecked feelings will become inner rage with destructive behaviors. If, we look at our kaleidoscopic society, you'll witness this without a shadow of a doubt, human behaviors are rampant and destructive with no remorse and no practical answers. Life at this present time is no different than a thousand years ago. We all say that history repeats itself, that's only because of our failure to really learn from it, rather than repeat the same thing that brought past pains and perilous endeavors. Since history hasn't changed concerning peoples' emotions, fears, and the means to be successful; then the blue-print of achievement doesn't need to be changed but enhanced. The paradoxes of life will always be present as long as there are human-beings. The paradox today and pastimes is the human rationale verses the animalistic nature. The use of skullduggery is very effective with these paradoxes, because it's no different than the hug and push syndrome. This leaves the person off-balanced or confused, and the tactical manipulator can be very exciting and intriguing. Humans always want what they can't have and turn down or do away with the banal. Having the skills of an orator, the mind of a philosopher, the ability to be secretive like a fraternal or sorority member, appearing very religious and spiritual, and having the honesty of a square dealing businessman makes it more easily to be trusted. The mind supersedes the body of emotions, but it can't do without the feelings or messages it conveys to the mind. Many of us fail to understand that our minds can create failures, without actually failing in reality. The mind is very acute to information and images, that have to be controlled or will run rampant with unproductive thoughts with internal images. Here's an example concerning women. A woman with understanding of her sexual prose can always have a monopoly or upper-hand of control on her admirer or lover to play on his psychology to draw him in. Once she has him hooked, locked and cocked on her whether by sexual skullduggery and psychological skullduggery, now she has the power to receive or take whatever he possess. One thing she can't do right off is give up the ass or her goods until he's totally under her control by all means. Then he'll do whatever it takes to keep her happy. So, emotions can be a great fuel to success like fuel to an aircraft-carrier, with great power to achieve. The fuel or passion of emotion has to be controlled or the mark of achievement will never get hit or reached. Our emotions are our energy mechanisms to carry us through our life with our daily strategies, tactics, defeats, and failure to overcome struggles with great endurance no matter what. The lack of understanding emotion and mind can be a great hindrance to have a better relationship, respectful colleagues on the job, a wonderful parent and child relation, and less havoc in society. Since, we're always encountering one without the other, we go through our lives on a daily bases having conflict with these paradoxes. This art has been achieved by the few that know how to used this paradox of mind verses emotion for the big gain or get the big pay-off. Many people bring their relationships from home to work, because many confide in their colleagues and open up with ease. Opening up easy only means that you're being effected by that emotion at that time, and blinded to whom you're opening up to. The person who's listening can become a potential lover or crutch through difficult times. Now, here's a relationship that wasn't planned, but since emotion was the ruler, and the listener was using their mind over emotion, then the listener becomes the confider over time. Like I've said before emotion that goes unchecked or uncontrolled will be a downfall and complication on the battle-field of life. Eye to eye contact is also a mental and emotional battle. The one that's able to give eye to eye contact without the slightest wink or without bowing the head first now is able to use skullduggery, because the person has been coined has a serious listener and a strong-minded individual. For centuries emotion has been identified with a woman, with many concepts that pertains to anger, lust, pleasure, understanding, and most of all ruthless seductive charming with great cleverness and feminine attraction. Mind has been synonyms with man, but here we'll give a few concepts to equate mind and man like for instance power, strength, wisdom, and the greatest concept is to be ruthless but prudent'. So here's where the motto or cliché' comes from, "behind every good man(wisdom), there's a good woman(understanding)." This cliché' demonstrates the oneness of man and woman, mind and emotion, working in harmony to bring about the desired goal or best out-come. Mind is for articulation, creativity, planning, stimulation and many uses etc,. Whereas emotion is for feelings of passion, inspiration, anger and many other human physical extremes and intense drives etc, to achieve. Religious leaders use these humanistic devices of emotion and mind concepts to create images, to hold sway over their members. Psychological skullduggery has been used by religious leaders for centuries, to create images mentally and physically of heaven and hell, which stirs the emotions to believe without proof. This form of skullduggery has been very effective since humans has been on planet earth. Many religious members have been brain-washed by their parents since childbirth to believe what their parents instilled in them. Then that belief becomes like their second nature, no matter how truthful , logical, and rational it goes against their emotions and mind to change. So, the religious leaders that understand this physiological and psychological make-up are able to capitalize and control their believers. Even though these religious leaders are in the business to teach people to be ever conscience of an All-Seeing Being, it goes to show how the masses of human-beings are frail and sheepish. When it comes to being a leader very few people are willing to take this responsibility, but the majority will condemn those that try with sincerity and willingness. With this truth you must understand that humans are fickle and hell-raisers by nature, whether social or political by all means. Another thing I must make mention about emotion and mind. When it comes to vengeance the mind is sleep or better yet dead to analyzes and plot a clever revenge. The human-breast is ferocious when it comes to getting what it desires. Whether it's freedom or vengeance, vengeance is so pleasurable to the avenger, it's like sex, drugs, and anything that gives the avenger, or normal person great pleasure. When the emotion is so strong with great fury the person will go all out no matter what the consequence is to obtain vengeance. So, getting on the other side of anyone can be a great danger for the one who fail to understand the human psychic. Misuse of skullduggery can lead a person or people as seeing themselves as victims of deceit and trickery and are willing to strike back like a beast, which is ferocious and potentially deadly. That's why politics, religion, philosophy, and war are major studies with all seriousness to the person who is seeking to be a leader or would be leader to rise from mediocrity to greatness. Because the human-being carries much will power within its nature, his strong desires to be free from poverty, daily-struggles, and deceit. Whether it's mind or emotion, each one of these human devices, can be a virtue or vice depending on each person disposition.

SHARP LIKE A RAZOR AND SLICK LIKE OIL

Now, we come to another concept on character, tactics and strategy for the leaders and would-be leaders. This section has been touched upon a little else where, but we will dive into this section dealing with audacity, cunning, manipulation, and taking on the character of the fox, chameleon, and bull. You may ask or ponder what does a fox, chameleon, and bull have to do with being sharp like a razor and slick like oil? We all know that a razor is definitely sharp and has to be handle with caution. Even the katana, the samurai's sword is very sharp to the touch and has to be handle with great caution. We know that oil is slick, slippery and it lubricates to remove rust spots or prevent water damage over a period of time. The sharpness of a razor here deals with the mind and retribution that a leader has to implement to hold his post of power or carve out an area to obtain power. The oil is the audacity to be very cunning, manipulative, and to perform skullduggery without being caught or held by the goodwill of the people or person as a fraud. This will cause the leaders' having power, wealth, status and leadership to crumble because the leader's lack of prudence and shrewdness. So, to remain in power or achieve power one has to be willing to put some very important things in perspective, before taking on this position or post which deals with the person or masses' civil liberties, their freedom of choice, their means to provide for their families, and their God given human rights. History has shown that any leader that use tyranny, terror, and brute force of all kinds lost their throne, because the people rose up at all cost to get what they felt was their human right, and freedom of choice concerning their daily lives. Another thing that history will inform us that, when any leader was held a cheat, fraud, selfish, and greedy, the people rebelled against their leaders. Even today we see the same thing is happening between the leaders and the people. History is repeating itself because of the lack of prudence with today's leaders. Majority of leaders or would-be leaders want fame. They fail to understand that the capacity of resentment and fickleness of other people and their protégés' run rampant in their hearts and minds at all times. So, in order to be a leader certain morals have to be seen by the people as honest. Since people are fickle by nature, it's better to some old ways and create changes that are beneficial for the people, and the people will hold the leader in high esteem and the leader will remain in power. Here's where another problem will cause tension or division within the walls of the leaders and their protégés and among the elite. The elite will press for the people to be heavily taxed and pressured to the higher-ups agenda, which lead to lost of freedom for the people. That's why I've mentioned before that leaders will have to be prudent and cognitive of their powerful elite circle's competence and loyalty. Many people fail to study human behavior and it's comparison to animals. Without rationality humans would behave as though they were animals. Learning and studying the ways of the fox is one way to recognize unwanted harm or dangers that lurk beneath the surface of sight. The fox has the ability to sense ambush, and scheme. That's why having the mind like a razor is like having the abilities of the fox. That's why shrewdness and skullduggery is an art, with the character of the fox is very pertinent. The chameleon is equivalent to the people's fickleness that dwells deep in the human anatomy and psyche. Leaders and would-be leaders must learn the ways and understand the chameleon's adaptability to change with change to hold power and keep the throne. Always being able to maneuver will give you more means to deceive and make power-plays to be above and beyond the norm. The character of the bull is all strength, boldness, territorial and power to achieve. It also, can be a pitfall of destruction with no cognition to stop or slow down. Any leader or would-be leader that uses the character of the bull, without the least amount of discretion and prudence will be the cause of his or her own down-fall and failure. Leaders have to implant in the peoples' minds, that the people's freedom and livelihood is the most important issue. This give room for the deceiver to use psychological skullduggery with razor sharpness, with acute cleverness and foresight. Whenever anyone is able to see trouble or unwanted guess from a foe, you should put oil on their path to cause the unwanted foe to fall and lose their balance(hypothetical). The concept of oil should be your deceptive tactic and power-play to be untouched by any means and by whomever tries to come and take what's yours. Long as you're willing to use these instruments of skullduggery like a razor to handle your foe, you can always be able to use your razor in peace for a nice clean shave, and use your oil to unbalance any unwanted enemy with deception, so that you can always have oil for your body and hair to shine. Ha, Ha! Knowing how to use the attributes or ways of the fox, is to be crafty, prudent, shrewd and aware of the unexpected; those who have reached the top, understood the way of the fox is the way to achieve with out interruption from foes and fools. So, use your mind like a razor, which is mental cleverness and the slickness of oil, which are tactics and strategies, without them will be your own demise or your means to rise.

Money and Fools

Money and fools will one day be separate like the East and the West. Better yet money and fools is like oil and water in a glass. The glass is the human, the oil is the money slipping out of the person's hands, and water is the refresh- ness that money can give and bring to the wise who can contain money. (Money will always remain in the hands of those people, who know what to do with money, and how to keep money flowing for their benefit and lifestyle.) People that have millions of dollars understand the concept of investing, networking, and courage. Financial education is imperative to remain financially stable and free. Fools are consumers, consumers, consumes, and wonder why they don't have money. Fools with money sooner or later will be a fool without money, because it will be in the hands of the rich or those who know what to do with money. Fools try and desire to look rich, with large capacity of things that have no value, investing or selling potential, and no incentive effect. Fools don't know anything about cash flow, and they should because money is flowing out of their hands continuously. But since they are fools, their minds operate on stupidity and wants. Fools with money will always benefit the person with a plan and desire to have more money. Those that work for money will never have enough money for their needs and wants. Powerful economical manipulators continue to engrave the laws and status for success and control. So, the fool continues to go through life blaming others for not having money. A fool is like a jack-ass, but much dumber and stubborn to change. Learning is imperative to know how to use money. There are those of us who know the value of money. That person understands what it takes to get rich and will one day be rich. Psychological skullduggery is a way and means to getting rich, staying wealthy and powerful. Business tycoons have a track record of making money and being honest, which also give them means to perform skullduggery. Many business tycoons and politicians are in cahoots with one another for more wealth, status, power and control. This is a major strategy to empower themselves and force the smaller businesses to either collapse or emerge with the super-players. This will give the powerful more power at the expense of the smaller business that needs the super-power to stay afloat. Whenever a person is in desperate need of the person with more power, there's precautions that need to be considered.

The stronger has to make that the weak, weaker in order to stay stronger to remain in control. If, not the strong will no longer have the power to remain the controller and power-player. No productive business has any business emerging with a power base that's able to wipe it out of existence. If any business that's able to stay in business without the need to emerge must do so at all cost. If not, that business will be it's own downfall, because of that powerful player rose through the ranks by the use of skullduggery, having billion of dollars to carry and strategically reorganize, implement productive networking, and the use of aggressive propaganda with tactical advertising. Fools think that having money is what it's all about. The wise has knowledge about what money can do, will do , and able to do because everything and everybody can be bought. For example, if you've only generated $50,000 for several years, and some business tycoon comes and offers you $250,000 for your business or talent, will you turn it down? The wise will search or look for leverage with this offer, and the naïve person will leap without thinking and wind up back in the same spot. The point I'm making is that the majority of us will jump at the first chance to have more and make more money. Having more constitute the core of the human make-up, whether it's a desire to have more money, time, knowledge, and understanding. It's the natural make-up of the human-being. Money comes from financial ideas that are implemented to generate money. The ideas have to be put to work and practice with great effort to achieve. Another thing about the fool, is they'll complain about getting up every morning to go to work for someone else, but don't have the slightest idea what to do to have their own thing. Working on a job is someone else's vision, which the fool depends on for their meager existence. Only a fool will try to consume much of nothing with a small amount money to survive. Propaganda is another art form of skullduggery performed with great accuracy, to target the public to buy, fear, stress, worry and follow the protocol set by the ones that understand skullduggery. Propaganda is a very effective means to obtaining power and remaining powerful. There's an old cliché' that says that "the fool with money is the rich man's greatest asset" and it still holds true today. Becoming a CEO or entrepreneur has nothing to do with universities, colleges, and trade schools. These are systematic curriculums set up by the powerful ones. The powerful leaders know what skullduggery can do to the minds of those that can be brain-washed with so-called education. The reality of entrepreneurship is more of an inner calling and desire to fulfill one's self by all means to be one's own boss. Those that are willing to get and have more money are willing to take chances for great economical advances. These chances may be scams, cunning, and manipulation on the marks. These marks are too blind to see and recognize that skullduggery is being performed on them for their money. Bankruptcy is a form of scam with a twist of skullduggery use by the elite and CEOs to get millions of dollar bonuses. This causes the business to file bankruptcy without giving the employees their share, because there's isn't any shares or service package to be given by the business. So, in essence only the fools believe that it's safe working and depending on someone else, when the majority of CEOs don't have the least consideration for their employees hard work.

Religious leaders know that keeping the people brain-washed under the guise of holiness is a great benefit to their establishment. If you look today you will see numerous places of worship on every corner. These religious leaders are setting up worship-houses like franchises. With all these places of worship, life is becoming more dangerous and treacherous. That's only to say that someone is not doing there job of saving lives or really doesn't know how to save lives. Many religious institutions are making more money now, than they ever have in their whole lives, because the people or members are giving their hard earn dollars to these religious chameleons. The ancestors knew how to invoke the spirits to work in their favor, and grant them the substance they needed to build on their wisdom, knowledge, and impeccable understanding of spiritual liberties, morals, poverty, and protection from their enemies. Today the religious leaders are teaching their members to remain weak and effeminate. These members believe in a magical god. Believing that the Great Providence will work wonders without the slightest effort on their part, which is stupefied and ludicrous. When people are this docile and sheepish, skullduggery is not even necessary. Only a little flattery, smiles, and more propaganda with an air of belief shows that you know what you're doing is all that's needed. Religion, politics, warfare, and businesses are imperatives studies to control these institutions. Studying human nature will grant the researcher or leaders of these studies to obtain power and wealth at the expense of those who fail to know how or fear obtaining greatness. By nature grants all things to reach its peak either physical or economical before it declines. Many people seek to have millions of dollars or just to have financial stability, but the fool fails to understand that with a small amount of money, a plan, an idea, and audacity, it can happen. But one has to be willing to do the unimaginable thing at times to achieve this glory. In our times compared to ancients days, when great men took education seriously, whether is was politics, warfare, law, rhetoric, grammar, religion, philosophy, and music which was mandatory to cultivate mental power, wealth, leadership, discipline and obedience. Education today has made man, and I must say this with no delusions, effeminate!! Women have become very vigorous, which has cause humanity to be in a disgruntle and despicable state of affairs, because of the inferiority complex of most men today. So, there's no reason to look for the Great Providence to grant great things to the weak, docile minded creatures that fail to witness this phenomena world of creation and their connection with it. Bottom line for any leader or would-be leader, he or she must understand how to use psychological skullduggery to obtain money, wealth, power, and seriously re- educate themselves on how to lead. This is the only study that has to be done with all seriousness to understand the art of skullduggery, which is very much necessary to remain in power. "You must understand the nature of humans, by starting with yourself first and foremost. Then, you'll see the art of how humans are, and not how they should or ought to be!!"

GIVERS, TAKERS AND MANIPULATORS

From childhood, we have always been taught that giving is better than receiving. We were told that if we gave and not expected anything in return; we would somehow in the end be blessed with much more than we gave. This is especially practiced upon religious, timid and tolerant minded people. Patiently they wait, giving all that they have, for the rewards of a free cheerful-heart. Care-free givers never get what they feel they deserve. This foolish teaching is only beneficial for the takers and manipulators. True givers will give and keep giving. Takers will take until there is nothing left to take. Manipulators will take from you and make you feel as if you received something in return. In essence you have learned at the expense of being naïve and too timid, that giving isn't what it's all cracked up to be. To be a taker is better than giving with the silly hopes of receiving what you didn't ask for before you gave. Manipulators know well that you have to receive something in order for them to keep getting what they need and want. So, the manipulators apply their craft with prudence and seductive motives. Takers are basically bullies or better yet operate with tyrannical motives. Prudent takers take what's offered and also by the use of psychological skullduggery they work on the hearts and minds of the givers. Anything that isn't worth having, the masters of skullduggery will not apply their trade and craft. When the art of skullduggery is understood with acute accuracy, you don't have to force anyone to do anything for you or give you anything by force. Because of the use and art of skullduggery, this promising art will reward the user of it every time. This art of manipulation and skullduggery has put primate rulers, leaders, business tycoons, great investors, war generals in primate arenas of greatness from ancient times to the present. Some business men have tried to use this art but failed. Because of today's greed, humans are failing to see what great men of past times have done to achieve and reign for many years. Men in olden days knew that greed will cause a great man to be murdered or removed from his or her throne. Today people want fame instead of power! Wanting fame only forces one to be greedy and tyrannical and never being able to see when to stop or change their tactics and strategies. Greed feeds the human emotion. It never satisfies the human ambitions, lascivious, and carnivorous nature of the humans today. How many times must I say that you must, you must, with all accuracy, prudence, seriousness, and with mindful ability understand what to do and never do, when deceiving anyone for big gains and big pay-offs. Cheerful givers are moralist, soft-hearted, and effeminate types of people. To be held a liar or cheat in their eyes of the person or persons will be your downfall. They're forced to seek judicial aide to prosecute you to the fullest. It only means that you didn't know what you were doing and fail to be prudent in the art of deception. Greedy takers and stupefied manipulators are showing and teaching the cheerful givers to be more aware of this art over time. When the cheerful givers become less and less givers in the world, that only means more mayhem in society. Masters of skullduggery know how to receive well from the givers, take what the givers offer with pleasure, and manipulate according to the givers understanding with the demeanor of great regards. Even in the olden days the wealthy took every precaution concerning their sons and daughters future when it came to marriages. The wealthy made sure that their son or daughter, took the hand of the giver who was rich or wealthy when offered their daughters or sons in marriage, and the parents were the manipulators to always keep wealth, power and royalty in their families at all cost. To this day this practice is mandatory among the wealthy concerning marriages and power. The mediocre and fools don't practice this form of marriage and wealth, that's why they remain without money, bad credit, and lack financial prudence. But over time some of these givers learn to be takers and manipulators for wealth, status, and rise above their mediocre lifestyle. Hardships can be a great motivator to the person that's fed up and willing to make a change, and be on the other side of the playing field. To be a giver of skullduggery, and a taker of the profits and proceeds, and continue to be a great manipulator to maintain is the present playing-field. Marriages and relationships is a give and take, but at times they both manipulate one another, when one feels like the other isn't behaving according to their love and the honesty of the relationship. Givers and takers are forever embedded to one another, because the paradoxes of life. These paradoxes isn't no different than hot and cold, wet and dry, and life and death. Only the manipulators understand this cycle of life, so they learn to give a little just to receive more. Who would ever think that the forefathers or the givers of the Constitution, understood the human-nature's pursuit for happiness, and freedom would be taking from the very people it was design for? As time goes by each one us, whether giver, taker and manipulator will sooner or later will switch roles, if one just looks and study human nature closely and see the phenomenon of this cosmic order. Givers, takers and manipulators will always thrive in the blood of humans. Either by their dispositions or by their up-bring and their education.

Ruthlessness and Its Means

Are the things we're witnessing ruthlessness or stupidity? What about the man that molests or rapes his 9yr old daughter, the dope fiend beats an elderly lady, then robs her, and the teacher having sexual relations with his/her students. What about the politician that gets caught embezzling and money laundering, the religious leaders running a prostitution ring within their temples, the CEOs getting $100 million dollar bonuses and then file bankruptcy, and the stock investor goes broke and murders his entire family. What about the college students that's on a killing spree throughout the country. Is the ruthlessness or stupidity?

Being ruthless always had a subject and objective means or, in other words a cause and an effect. Being ruthless has nothing to do with uncontrolled anger, destruction of anyone and everything, murdering the innocent without cause, or carrying out a plan for fame and game. Having a plan with great audacity, being tenaciously unwavering, and being courageous to reach the goal one has set out for oneself is being ruthless. Before entering in to this articulated designed mode of being. You have to know the means of how to project this state of being. Knowing what's at stake if one fails, knowing where, when, and whom to act upon with this ruthless attitude. If you study history very closely, you'll witness those leaders that utilize treachery, pillage, and murder which was their means of reigning. However, their reign was short lived because of their lack of prudence of knowing how to be ruthless. Being or using this articulated form of ruthlessness should only be used for order, control, obedience, and to put in the minds of the subordinates, that you are not to be crossed by any means, without a price of a losing their status or retribution. Being determined about something, but yet stepped on, not taken seriously, and questioned to often is an indication you're not being ruthless. Ruthlessness carries an air of authority. Having authority comes with leadership abilities, which many people are afraid of implementing. War generals were ruthless not only when fighting their enemies, but also with their soldiers. These great war generals knew that without this attitude their soldiers wouldn't have a chance to achieve victory. When carrying out a plan that's significant to your cause of achieving power and putting things in perspective you have to be ruthless.

That's only to show your seriousness and not to be taken for an effeminate person. No leader can be a leader nor can anyone rise from their mediocre means to greatness being effeminate person. Politicians use ruthlessness to keep order in society and when it comes to caring out plans strategically for the nations safety, and they should always be ruthless in preserving the freedom of the people with discretion . Any politician that finds ruthlessness uncalled should never enter politics. Being the head always required great demands on the body, whether that body be people, party of politicians, employees, sports players, and teachers over their students to bring about great strides of development. Ruthlessness is a must in order to rise above the normal status and to remain in power. Now, this attitude and form of virtuous state comes with prudence, intelligence, and an acute cognitive mind of knowledge on leading and obtaining the obtainable. Homicide detectives and interrogators are ruthless- diplomatic when it comes to solving crimes of deaths related to homicides. These detectives and interrogators also use psychological skullduggery on possible suspects, when they question their suspects to obtain evidence to solve their cases.

Using the art of psychological skullduggery with ruthlessness, is a person that's virtually on their way to greatness and achieving their goal. The person that uses these art form of skullduggery and ruthlessness is a person who conquering obstacles and drawing people in for their personal achievement. You should never mix ruthlessness with being a bully or anger. Bullying and uncontrolled anger are both forms of insecurities and emotional rage, which are very self-destructive. Let me digress for a moment with an example of ruthlessness and achieving a goal. Lets say for instance that you're determined to open a business, go to college for nursing or whatever you want to achieve, but you have friends and family members discouraging you, and speaking negatively about your personal goals. Now here's when you should be ruthless, to continue by all means to reach your goal. It's your personal fulfillment to achieve for yourself, to be somebody productive, and also live above mediocre status in a growing world that's demanding greatness. Only the ruthless minded person will reach their goals, become a great achiever and leader. Being ruthless also comes with the heart to be unremorseful when the situation calls for it. If you have a business and need to fire someone then so be it. (When it comes to your love ones whether it's your husband, boyfriend, wife, girlfriend and close associates, that needs to be cut off from you associating with them to reach your goals. You've got to be ruthless and cut their ass off with no remorse for doing it or instill in their minds that you're going to achieve your goal with them or without them point blank.) No ands, ifs, buts, or compromise can enter in this endeavor of greatness. To compromise is to open the door of hindrance, lack of energy, lost of time, lack of focus, and eventually no drive to rise above of the banal status of life. This ruthless state comes with an attitude. Basically, it is to have them kissing your ass right in the ringer, and have them elated about kissing your ass. If you can't do that or have them doing that, then kiss your goal good bye and kick your own ass for being effeminate and a coward, because that's where it's going down the drain. Opportunities don't come too often in a person 's life time to obtain or reach a certain level of greatness. So, you have to be relentless per se' to recognize and seize opportunities at the first sign they appear. If you're not able to recognize opportunities, then you have to be ruthless and make something happen for you in your favor. In my past, being a womanizing, being a player or playboy, my women had to be good for me, in order for me to be good to them. If they weren't good for me, then I couldn't be good to them. So, me associating with them discontinued no matter how she or they felt about it. You've got to be willing to step on few and kick as many in the ass, hypothetically speaking. To reach greatness or rise above your banal status, is what separates the weak from the strong, men from the boys, and ladies from the girls. Some say it takes guts, when you' re being ruthless. You don't feel or know you have guts until you're relaxed at the outcome of how things are operating in your favor. HA, Ha! You should never stay in the ruthless mode over long periods of time. This will dull your senses, because you're working overtime without rest and not having the means to see the outcome and re-evaluate your progress. Anyone working overtime without rest or time to re-evaluate themselves will be grouchy and strike at people that may be helpful to their progress. This will only slow down your progress. Now you're left entirely to your own mediocre vices and efforts to achieve your goal. You have to be psychologically equipped to carry out this form of attitude and tactic to reach the top or maintain your successful status. Another thing to consider is when you're associating with someone that's ruthless. You have to consider how you can use this person's passion of ruthless determination to move you up the scale of success. If you're rubbing elbows with anyone that's ruthless and you're the protégé', you have take a little strife and shit every so often. This tactic must be considered with acute prudence, more determination than the ruthless one, and playing the pawn for the gain and big-off; that comes with learning the game of obtaining power. Being over zealous without some things considered, will only lead you to become a tyrant and dispelled by many, which is your own downfall. Being a tyrant is monstrous, oppressive, and uncivil, but you can still achieve your goal. Not knowing how to be tyrannical with skullduggery will hinder or prevent you from achieving your goal. History has shown that anyone that uses the tyranny syndrome didn't last or reign long, and was over thrown or murdered by the people. Lack of psychological skullduggery with prudence, strategies, and tactics will never reward anyone that's desiring to become a leader, remain a leader or obtain power. I would like to present ruthlessness from another stand point when it comes to the street life and ruthlessness. Ruthlessness on the streets is similar to that in corporate business, war and political warfare. When it comes to the drug arena, you have the drug kingpin, the pusher, the peddler, and the addict. This drug arena exist on every street corner, in every major city in America. It has in the past and even still today. The kingpin supplies the whole nation with drugs from coast to coast. The kingpin is the manufacture that supplies the pusher, the pushers, then sells to the peddler, and finally the dope-addict gets their fix at a cost. The drug kingpin is the CEO with various illegitimate investments concerning drugs and minimum legal investments . The pusher is more of an administrator of the streets; to the peddlers in this arena of business to continue his operation. The peddlers is the worker, which depends on the higher ups in this operation, and finally the customer is the addict. Now, here's when this operation becomes a warfare that you would read about in the papers or see on the evening news. The Kingpin is invisible not able to be touched, because he remains out the lime-light of the business. The battle that will come in to play, will be the pusher and the peddler. (If the peddlers rise to the level of a pusher in the same location, of that present pusher. Like all major businesses location, location, and location is very important to the survival of that business. When these two street level money- makers are operating in the same area, and the pusher loses sells and money, because the peddler has become a major player in the drug arena; this will lead to a hostile form of negotiating for one or the other to relocate or the street death sentence will be the final decision. Now-days some become stool-pigeons(rats or snitches). When you have to protect your means and your instrument for your survival at all cost, the way of the beast, which is ferocity and ruthlessness will be the means that justify this action. Many will say, "How is this similar to corporate-business, war and political warfare?" It's called getting rid of your competition or eliminating your opponent(not physical with bodily harm in the business arena) that hindrances the business progress. (No different from economical war profits, political solicitation for campaign funding, corporate scams, and pharmaceutical drug inventions for profit that has destroyed many lives.) Learning the attributes of the bull, is knowing how to be courageous, having audacity, and strength. Utilizing the way of the bull in all situations will never work or bring success. Ruthlessness is one source or bedrock and code of success, whether business, warfare, political, relationships, and mandatory decisions while in office and the means to never be conceived or thought as being weak, docile or sheepish.

SCAMS AND WHO GIVES A DAMN

Different types of scams have been happening to people since the beginning of time. Because of technology, it has made scamming much easier and sophisticated to the mark's appeal, which seems believable and convincing that this scam is legit. Many in the past and present have tried scamming for small gains, but fail to realize that many small scams only leave you to perform more scams; which only leave tracks for the feds and police officers to catch them in the act. Those that mastered the art of psychological skullduggery perform scams on a grand level. Like performing major credit card scams, scamming art galleries that have million dollar insurances on their art or copying the art of famous artists, which is a forgery and selling it for millions of dollars. Scamming jewelry store workers, by trying on many rings at time. This way the seller can't keep up with the scammers, then the scammers walk out with an expensive ring or rings to sell to the highest bidder on the streets. Real scammers that live by the art of the scam, always do their scamming where the stakes are worth the scam. Mainly, scoping out the businesses and persons before putting your plan into action is the scammers job. When these masters perform their task, they just lay-low and wait for things to cool-off. Because they got away with enough cash to lay-back or invest it in some profitable business, scamming has been utilized by street grifters, mitt-men games, political scams, businessmen, and the worst or most immoral religious scams. The scammers don't give a damn about who they're scamming, only the ones that got scammed and realized they were scammed gives a damn. Today we have wall-street scams, bank scams, internet scams, and the sophisticated business scammers, that's scamming people out of millions of dollars over-night or in a matter of hours. Why are there're so many willing victims of scams? It's our human nature that desires more, whether it's money, happiness, love, time, sex and a longer-life. So, it makes it easy for the scammer to pull off the scam with ease. The scammer that knows how to utilize the art of skullduggery, understands human nature and human psychology. Technology has advanced over the years, with mechanical eyes planted everywhere, and scammers are still scamming. No matter how advanced technology becomes remember this. It takes a man to invent technology, but the human psychology is the thing that invented it and brought it to fruition. So, just like it took a human to invent technology, it also will take a human-mind to break the code of the invention or mechanism over time. Why is it right for politicians and primate businessmen to perform scams and nothing happens, but a man that's deprived of an economical occupation and needs to feed his family is wrong? We need to understand that as long has there is humans there will be scammers. Humans are lazy and creatures of habit, so there will always be scammers. The psychology of scammers are realist. The scammers focus is on what they need and want now! Greed is one thing that causes some of these unsophisticated scammers to get caught. Where there's much greed, there's the lack of prudence, lack of control, and the art of scamming with complete discretion. The easiest way to scam anybody is to appeal to the person that's looking or desiring more for themselves. Scammers are suppliers of demand, with much knowledge on how and whom to scam. Some have went as far scamming casinos and marrying for money, which is a form of scamming. Scamming someone and creating an air emotion is the best scam, because it's scam proof. Drug-addicts scams for small things, but are very convincing and manipulative when scamming you. Pan-handlers are scammers too, with an outfit that looks like a hungry and starving person, but it as been known that 35% of the pan-handlers are not hungry and deprived of anything. It's the art of the scam that many are starting to perform for easy money. So, one has to have the eyes to see into things and not at things. Many of us have came across an magnificent offer, that seems too real to be true, but turned it down, because it seems to be other than what it appears to be. Learning the scam and the hoax of the scam game will prevent you from being the next dupe or victim of the scam from those that don't give a damn. Remember scammers come in all shapes and sizes. The best scammers are very sophisticated, articulate, well-groomed, have a smooth debonair effect, and very appealing, which helps to lower the guards of their victims. This is one of the major reasons why great scammers get-off and are able to apply their trade with ease, because of their so-called business attire. The scammers business is scamming day and night. Basically, to be a good scammer you have to learn and utilize the way of the fox and chameleon. Which is to adjust and change to the person's thoughts and feelings; you want the person to see things your way and to hook them or bait them in; according to the person's desires and wants to pull off the scam with ease. You make them feel like what they want and desire they can have, and to see things your way is much better and less complicated. Using their passion, desires, and greed against them, is how scammers get what they need and want. This is how you utilize the art of the scam. Scammers will get you sooner or later by hook or crook, but mainly with the art psychological skullduggery. "It's sad that many of us are so naïve and trust-worthy people, but that's human-beings for you. So, learn their ways!!"

BRAINS, GUTS, AND BRASS BALLS

Men and women that relinquish power always have been movers and shakers of the past and present world. The main reason they're movers and shakers, is because of their brains to implement a blue-print for power, guts to carry out the plan, and the brass balls, which is audacity and determination to make their goal fruition. Being effeminate you can't obtain power or step on the turf to play with real warriors. Politicians, CEOs, war-generals, and street hustlers don't operate on emotion. They're heartless when it comes to reaching the top or remaining on the pedestal of success. In this game of power being morally good can be detrimental to your means of achieving power and success. You should have the prudence to know when and not to be morally good, but you should have the guts and brass balls to be cruel when need be. Cruelty has its place, time, and purpose, when it should be utilize. Prudence is very important when implementing cruelty for the cause of success. Many historians and present writers have written on cruelty, but today cruelty has been misconstrued with being gruesomely barbaric and aggressive without acute insight. Many politicians and dictators in ancient times misused cruelty, and was murdered or dethrone by the behest of the people. Even religious leaders were and are cruel, clever, and determined to carry out their plan for their political and religious gains, which is to obtain power and maintain the status of power as long as possible. Many religious leaders of the past and present utilized more of their sexual balls for pleasure, which turned the people against them for immoral practices. Lack of prudent leadership skills will be the cause of any would-be leader to fail. If they would have put the art of psychological skullduggery into effect the people would be brain-washed, which will maintain your seat of power. Having brains, guts, and brass balls is like running a war or political campaign, which is to win by any means within the law of campaigning. Without the art of skullduggery you must understand, and know the laws of governing people; have to be followed with carefulness. When you use the tools of skullduggery, whether politicking, or during war, you must understand there's war crimes, and in business you should know the loopholes before engaging in deceit and trickery, which can bring you legal conflict or imprisonment, because you fail to know the rules and laws. You should have the brains to have powerful associates in high places for the future and to remain in power to reach your goal of power and status. It takes guts to get out there and network and recruit good and willing pawns to put your plan in effect. With the art of psychological skullduggery, you should make the plan seem as though it's both of yours, the person and you, but in reality it's your plan and goal to be achieved. Unless that person and yourself are working in cahoots to achieve the same goal of business enterprise, loyalty is very important for this successful endeavor between your associate and yourself. Now, if the person is willing to remain on your side with your success and their minimum achievement compared to yours, you should be cautious at all cost. People today are very vengeful and emotionally driven, without the care and thought of being thrown into jail or bringing their own demise. Having intelligence and cleverness is very much lacking today. Without prudence no matter how determined or willing you are to achieve your goal, that goal will never fruition. No one can achieve anything without the know how first, and the discretion of what's needed to bring the many in harmony to put the one thing and plan into effect. Just like the heading of this section is brains, guts, and brass balls all these parts have to work in harmony to bring this plan and goal to reality. One of these human mechanisms can't work without the use of the other two, to be a successful leader or would-be leader. You can have the brains and brass balls, to desire success, but without the guts to carry it out, it's all useless and a waste of energy. What's the use of wanting and desiring something, but yet afraid to go ahead like a shark or whale moving tenaciously; in the deep sea of life eating swiftly as it moves about for its survival. It takes brains, guts and brass balls to survive in a world of so many devils posing as angels. Not many people have the eyes to see the reality of human nature, and the actions of people today like in pastimes. It was imperative in ancient

times to study human behavior and animal characteristic and their similarities with human-beings. Without the study of human psychology and human behavior the art of psychological skullduggery is useless like a car without oil. The study of humans is a must and a ongoing study, until you are no longer in human form or don't have the mental ability to do so.

Psychological Skullduggery

I've made mention that psychological skullduggery is an art, of knowing how to deceive, manipulate, con, knave, and trickery. This art is all mental without the slightest form of emotion. It's a mind game; that's played seriously on your opponents for control, obtaining power, and having the strings to pull your puppets, without them knowing their strings have been pulled; by a master puppeteer that's pulling their strings. Leadership is another subject I've also brought to the surface. Leaders today have left their followers behind in the dark with blinders on. Any person or persons who is posing as a leader, and leave their followers behind is no longer a leader, but an individual seeking its own gratification. This goes to show that selfishness dwells deep within the human psychology and physiology. To utilize this art you must stay focus on your goal, your surroundings, and mainly who you are manipulating. This consist of listening well, and thinking three steps ahead of the given situation. Never get too far ahead of yourself when applying this art, because you will not be able to see the reality of what's taking place. Understanding and knowing the thoughts, behaviors, habits, like and dislikes, and seeing the person's actions will give you an indication of their psychology. With this information concerning your subordinate's psychology and actions. You should be able to gain control, an upper hand to put the person or persons to work with elation to perform any task within their capacity for you. Psychological skullduggery is the way war-generals, warriors, political campaigners, businesses, players of women, and female players have obtained their goals. Anyone that's seeking to rise above their mediocre status has to utilize this art form of deception like great men and women through out history. The present would-be leaders have lost the blue-print of this great art. The citizen are losing so much of their possessions they've worked hard to obtain by new laws that's lawfully consists of taking. These leaders today are yelling democracy which only leads to perniciousness. History has revealed the seriousness of skullduggery that was utilized by rulers, monarchs, principalities, and princes, that democracy only leads to one thing and one thing only, "Anarchy." Majority of leaders who have obtained his or her post of power have utilized deceit, but skullduggery is for the selected few. Skullduggery has a form of deceit in its blue-print of power positioning, but its not the bedrock or the core of its workings. To be greatly deceitful without the slightest indication of cheating and cunning is to perform this art of psychological skullduggery. Prudence and skullduggery go hand and hand. If you're a lazy minded individual then you can forget about this art of psychological skullduggery. This art is for the serious minded individuals who seek power, control, and to rise above their normal playing field of life. Having a game plan and knowing the game you're playing must be taken into consideration. For example, the rules that consists of playing chess are not the same rules that can be applied to the game of checkers. You must know the game you're playing before you learn the rules of that game, then you play to understand how to create a strategy to win. The better you become with all seriousness, is the way to utilizes cunning and deceit to out maneuver your opponents. Then the psychology of knowing that deception works when undetected. This should show you that the art of skullduggery has to remain undetected in order to go far and obtain the obtainable that you seek to possess. If its hard for you to keep secrets, then forget about mastering the art of psychological skullduggery. Secrets are powerful information that's only able to be kept by the strong minded individuals. For example, I'll digress for a moment. Have you ever been told something, and felt like damn with all excitement and elation when you heard it, and then later you told someone else what the other person had revealed to you in all secretly. The person that told you the secret doesn't actually know the person you spilled the secret to. Some people have blurred out secrets under the influence of alcohol or angry at the person for some underline reason like betrayal and back-stabbing, and revealed the secret or secrets. I only put this small scenario to show you the power of knowing something that the other person doesn't brings a form of self elation and power. With untold secrets this is a way to gain the upper hand, because of the information that's been revealed. So, don't spill it or reveal it, use it, only if it can be utilized for some form of power positioning. Here's one of my personal philosophies of life, " His true secrets will go down with him to the grave, and leave with you the mask, when they bury him with his smooth manipulating ass." So, use this art with great audacity and prudence to obtain the richness of life, and fuck all that good guy finish first bullshit. The good guy son-of-bitch will not obtain shit in this world, but bills, head-aches, debt and more debt, and funky memories. Psychological skullduggery will reward the man or woman that masters this art with determination, prudence, resilience, tenacity, boldness to act, and patience to move with rhythm to carve out a playing field that will reward you for a lifetime, and your children's' children. It has rewarded those before us that sat on the thrones of power that have been passed down for generations to generation till this present day. You must understand this art before you can get rewarded by her ways and tactics to achieve. There's no short cuts and getting around this art. Those that have inherited seats of power, wealth, and status without the slightest understanding of this art lost their seat of power and prestige that their fore-parents and parents worked very hard to obtain with diligence and dedication to obtain their wealth and status.

I'm not here to speak on what we should do to make this world better. You have a committee of world politicians and political-advisors meeting year after year and day after day, theses so-called men and women of intelligence have been meeting and dialoguing for years and things are getting worse for the citizens and nations around the world. What the hell could they be discussing? Remember that behaviors and actions only show the thoughts of a people. Presidents and Congressmen have always said, "God Bless America!" Could the God of Heaven, Mercy, Compassion and Love grant these type of blessings? To understand the core and the heart of politics is to understand psychological skullduggery, and to truly understand psychological skullduggery, and its implications it to truly understand politicking. Seeing the depths of skullduggery you witness the games these religious leaders psychologically use in seducing their sheepish members to give their hard earned dollars. Becoming business and economical literate you will be able to recognize the manipulation of skullduggery performed by business tycoons, and their political associates who they strategically administer these psychological practices. With that having been said, it's the lack of understanding psychological skullduggery, the lack of prudence, and human fickleness that's failing us as a whole. These practices we should be observing very carefully to understand, the mental state of this beautiful nation, that's slowly beginning to lose her beauty from within by her own citizens; they have come to embrace her with all adoration. Is psychological skullduggery bringing her downfall? Or is it the miss use or lack of understanding of skullduggery with too much deceit without prudence? We all tell lies, we all perform acts of deception, when it suits us to deceive. The only thing is that many of us really don't know how to tell beautiful lies to pull off the hoax. That's why I've made mention over again and again, the importance of the psychology that has to be embedded, within the person or persons that's trying to deceive for a big pay-off or gain the upper-hand on the chess-board of life. Skullduggery is an implementation of constructive deceit. It's not a loose end strategy and tactic that's left untied. Neither does the implementer of this art burn all their bridges. They've always kept certain bridges standing that can be later utilized if need be. With prudence you'll know which and what bridges should be burned without the slightest hesitation.

Remember this is an art, which means no sloppiness can never be injected into this great art. All great art has air of prudence, grandeur of articulation, respect, keenness, and value that reward the artist and the later comer to possess this art that's priceless. The best way to use psychological skullduggery is to listen to the other person carefully. Then psychologically use words that stimulate their minds, rhythmically tantalizing their emotions, and scenarios that are heart felt with great clarity for them to believe without doubt. To be a master of this art, you must think like a fisherman. Every serious fishermen knows what type of bait is used in order to catch certain types of fish. You have to know the water you are fishing in, and the grounds you're trending -plus the people's thoughts. You must speak with them in order for them to see, and understand your ways of seeing the world. Implant this art with prudence into their minds. Once they agree to what you are saying is logical and right, you got them. Apply the art with emotion they desire and feel. Whatever you inject into their soul, mind, and heart is the way they feel about you from that point onward. Also get the person to reveal or brag about themselves, and talk with all freedom to speak about their past pains and gains. Listen carefully to what makes them happy or sad, and even understand what pisses them off. The more you know and understand about a person, the easier it is to use this art for power and control. Psychological skullduggery has to be deeply injected like a needle of medicine within their soul of thinking, and feeling in order to control them with easy. Puppet-masters use words to sway you to their ways of seeing, believing, and feelings about any situation or event.

Some charities use psychological skullduggery to swindle people for their money. They use advertising very strategically to implement the plan to make millions of dollars. Some of these charities use TV commercials; showing the unfortunate ones in desperate need of medical supplies, food, shelter, and clothing aide. Fraudulent charities use the art of skullduggery to manipulate your emotions, and mind with sympathetic ways of thinking. These charities play on people's feels with a twist of religious jargon "Give that you may receive many blessings", and many fall for this religious hype without the slightest thought. The NEWS media are the greatest system or media moguls that use psychological skullduggery strategically, tactically, and prudently to shape, and mold the minds of watchers world-wide. The NEWS media can make the victim look like the predator, and make the predator look like the victim. It all depends on the story that will bring great profits and shape the world minds for control concerning the event or events. The media moguls can make the guilty look or appear innocent, and have you believe the innocent is guilty. When the law says "Every person is innocent till proven guilty." Psychological skullduggery can shape your mind to condemn anyone without proof or facts. Politicians implement this art with critique rhetoric, orator skills, and to have you believe their plan for the country will be better than the last president, governor or congressman, during voting and campaign seasons. Daily world destructions and catastrophes you see are being orchestrated by masters of skullduggery to put their plans in effect. Whenever you get some one to see things your way without the least amount of resistance, then you have the skills of psychological skullduggery. If, you encounter some resistance or struggle, it only means that you haven't achieved this art. Another way to use psychological skullduggery is to utilize reverse psychology. Most people are able to see or recognize reverse psychology, that's why I greatly advise the student of this art to use skullduggery with the air mystery and manipulation. Whenever you find yourself talking too much become aloof and silent. Men and women use psychological skullduggery on one another all the time. This is one of the main reasons why relationships are breaking-down, because each one are trying to rule or control the other without the slightest know how.

So, I say walk lightly, be very insightful, listen attentively and deeply, remain silent unless you have to speak, make sure the words you speak be the skills of an orator, and in all a surety have the mind of psychological skullduggery.

POEMS OF PAIN AND PROSPERITY

Bloody Minded

Check the course of human events,
Rapidly bodies are being tossed in the burial trench.
Humans are fighting for their life from the womb
to the tomb,
Politicians are treating people like dust and they're
the broom.
Many drug users are street rock-stars,
The use of drugs is spreading like a wild-fire.
Only a few eyes are looking to the Eastern-star,
Staying focused and humble is the way to go far.
Bloody minds is a serious epidemic,
Greed is causing much human havoc.
Love is hard to find,
Evil is planted in the breast with bloody minds.
Trying to stay focus with tenacity,
Living in a heartless society is a difficult possibility.
Racism and violence is the essence of daily misery,
Politicians talking about fighting a war in the East,
What about the war on these American streets.
The police suppose to protect cities and
communities,
But they are contributing to violence and brutality.
Evil eyes and a dark heart is where it all starts,
A bloody mind will justify the cruel effective parts.

Will Be

He didn't ask to be here, but he's a man,
He sees a world where no one gives a damn.
Mother is his god on earth,
Unconditional love she gave since his birth,
A young man being taught cruel ways,
To survive he says fuck a Judgement Day.
If you teach a man to be a crook,
Every chance he gets something will be took.
Give him the reason to be a street-dealer,
He'll sell it to your mother and sister.
Show him how to be a pimp or player,
Another woman hooked on the words of soothe-
sayer.
Teach him to be hated,
Another life will horribly masqueraded.
Give him a reason to be worthless and hopeless,
He'll be some where doped mentally coasting.
Display the reason he shouldn't trust you,
Next time he'll turn his back and say fuck you.
Give him the reason to treat you like a bitch,
You'll get disrespect and treated like dung on a
stick.
If you give a man a reason to live in the dark,
He'll be the man with no care in his heart.
However a man sees his means to survive in his
society,
Today and tomorrow is what he'll be.

Men and Women

Men fail to know and women fail to understand,
Each one doesn't know their nature for unity to
stand.
Men's nature is to receive and women's nature is to
give,
The cycle of life to live.
Women are to know how they want to be treated,
Men must understand how to be loved and needed.
Today men are like women and women are acting
like men,
They both are causing this world to spin in a
destructive world wind.
Evil minds are responsible for this,
The devil always had a group to perform his
evilness.

A Need For A Change

History says a great teacher turned water into wine,
Water was transformed into another liquid kind.
When are you parents and so-called adults are
going stop lieing,
These kids are repeating the same process and are
mentally dieing.
Have you ever seen a reindeer fly in the sky,
Or rabbits lay eggs, why?
Most humans are like stale water,
You can smell the deadly slaugther.
Our kids are a reproduction of what we produce,
Or even what we fail to do.
Change is hard but it's necessary,
Even climate changes for us to have bananas and
strawberries.
Many people say there's nothing wrong with
intoxicating drinking,
Look at these daily deaths because of this ignorant
thinking.
A Divine transformation,
Is the only way to save a nation.

Everyone Aren't Who They Say They Are

There once was two boys who went to the same
school,
The oldest boy thought he was extremely kool.
The younger boy admired the oldest boy,
He felt mature and accepted with great joy.
The oldest boy always said the right thing,
He made the young boy feel like they were a team.
The oldest boy always conned to the youngest,
And always said "Damn he's the dumbest."
After many trials of trying to fit in,
The young boy felt the sin, from deep within,
So, the young boy told the oldest he couldn't do
wrong things again,
The oldest then said, "I thought you were my
friend."
The younger boy replied, "I thought you were to,
but that's the end."
Some people can make you feel like a star,
Sooner or later you'll see who they really are.

Technology Versus Psychology

The present world has advanced greatly,
When you look at it materially.
Can technology bring true peace and satisfaction,
Only if the human desires material things with
great attraction.
Technology has its purpose and good use,
But it's becoming the same thing that destroys me
and you.
The human psychology is the greatest asset,
Nothing in creation can come pass it.
Psychology creates Kings, Queens, and bastards,
Man is moving without thinking and life is a
mental hassle.
Psychology should be used for the betterment of
world technology,
The ancients understood the power of human
psychology.
Weak minds believe in destructive technology,
The misuse of human psychology,
Will be the destructive use of technology.

Reason and Mind

One night Reason was upset with Mind,
Mind accused Reason for not joining him at this
moment of time.
Reason didn't get out of character,
Reason saw why not to lose character was better.
Mind was out of control, because of the five treasures,
Reason spoke and rose, because there wasn't
equilibrium with the measures.
Mind demanded his moment to feel good,
Reason without feeling was above that what's below,
so he understood.
Mind became fierce with anger,
Reason left because he knew the danger.
Mind neglected the admonishment of Reason,
Moments later Mind was caught in a worldly
treason.
Mind called out to Reason to appear,
Reason spoke, "I'm always up here."
Mind asked Reason, "How can we stop these
worldly confusions?"
Reason said, "By leaving out illusions.
That's a world of hell and confusion,
When you Mind become one with me,
And me Reason become one with thee,
Then, we will live in peace and harmony,
Our Great Divine One willed for it to be Eternal
Unity."

Ignorance and Intelligence Unites

One day Ignorane was standing on the corner with
a gun in his trousers,
Intelligence asked Ignorance, "what's this all
about?"
Ignorance replied, "Shut up I'm trying to focus, so
stop!"
Intelligence stated, "You know what you're thinking
isn't right,"
Moments later an innocent lady came in sight.
Ignorance saw the lady getting out of her car,
Ignorance with great speed ran, as he watched from
afar.
He yelled at the lady demanding her jewelry and
money,
The lady saw his anger and her life ending in
moments,
He shot her in the mid-section,
He stole her car and was speeding through every
intersection.
When Ignorance arrives at his apartment building,
Intelligence started screaming, "What the hell are
you doing?"
Intelligence continued, "You're bring our
foundation to ruin."
Ignorance saw the evening News and became very
disturbed,
The world was getting the N*E*W*S and the word.

Ignorance told Intelligence, "I'll make a move when it's dark,"
Intelligence said, "No matter when or where our soul will pay for this demonic heart."
Moments later Ignorance was on the run speeding down the free-way,
Not paying attention he was stop by a cop right away.
Ignorance was perspiring with great intensity,
He started suttering through his guilt and nervous mentality.
When the police asked for his identity,
Ignorance sped off driving through communities.
Ignorance was eventually caught and went to jail,
The Judge gave him an expensive bail.
He started contemplating while sitting in his cell.
Intelligence spoke, " you still haven't lost the war,
Because of who and what you are,
You can still shine like a star."
Ignorance fell on his knees and said, "Please Lord of Eternity,
Help and save me before I stand in front of your Judgement seat."
Intelligence spoke, "Become one with the cosmos,
And ignorance will be no more."

Building the Corner-Stone

Man was created in his Maker's image,
Yet the Creator wasn't finished.
Adam was the start of spiritual forming,
Noah builds the Ark because the flood of ignorance
is coming.
Abraham was the wisdom of many nations,
Sodom and Gormorah brought its damnation.
Israel was Jacob's birth-right,
Moses was initiated by the Egyptian wisdom day
and night.
Joshua was given strength from the Divine Light,
David became king by the Eternal Mighty Sight.
Solomon completed his temple after seven years,
Job was ninety degress with godly fear.
The Lord spoke to the prophet Jeremiah,
Ezekiel revealed the wicked will die.
Daniel understood visions and dreams,
Then Jesus son of Mary comes on the scene.
Later Muhummad of Arabia becomes another
world Savior,
Each stone needs the chisel and plumb,
Building the corner-stone is man's realm.

That Nagging Woman

This ill-tempered woman, is always arguing about something,
Thinking she knows everything and yet our world is crumbling.
Always pointing the finger ready to blame,
She feels like burns from the raging flames.
Finding a reason for me to change,
When I'm the one doing productive things.
If you treat her like a Queen,
That hateful bitch will really get mean.
Trying to compromsie with this stubborn female,
Is like setting and talking with Satan in Hell.
She gets really upset when I'm gone,
She roars like Hell when I come back home.
My love for her is high that it soars,
She's lose like a street whore.
There's nothing I can do to balance this affair,
I sit on the roof-top of my house,
To get peace from that dangerous mouth.
No matter how I try to be fair,
Yet this isn't going anywhere.
The more I try to let her know what I'm seeing,
She always telling me what she wants and dreaming.
Now, I'm in the desert of no man's land of wandering,
Just to get away from that nagging-ass woman.

Moses and The Promise

Moses, where's the promise land?
"Follow me and you'll find it man."
Moses, why are we in this desert facing death and
extreme fatigue?
"Did you think it was easy to enter the Holy Place
promised to you and me."
Moses, where's the water to refresh?
"Deep within life's conquest."
Moses, why are you climbing Mount Sinai?
"To reach the peak of the Highest Science."
Moses, why did you marry an outsider?
"Binah and me is the only way to see the universe
much wider."
Moses, why are Aaron and you debating?
"Limited understanding and strength is always
complicating."
Moses, why are you confronting Pharaoh?
"That you may understand life's fears and sorrows."
Moses, why are you putting us through these trials
of Hell?
When you get to that Blessed land of Heaven, you'll
see the Most Holiest place to dwell."
Moses, where's the Promise Land you promised me?
"Above your head and beneath your feet."

CONCLUSION

Now, I must conclude this blue-print and art of psychological skullduggery. This art is being utilized today with many people not even realizing it. Don't get me wrong there are some sincere politicians, business leaders, Ceos, police-officers, teachers, parents, war generals, and religious leaders that are really trying to make this world better. Many of us who have children would hate for anybody to do any type of harm to our love ones. This is what most people fail to consider, they would hate for someone to harm their love ones, but they're harming and destroying someone else's love one. Many leaders today fail greatly to understand history and people today. Any leader that used tyrannical tactics over a long periods of time became the victim of his own method. War generals that fail to see the economical strain they put on the people for long war campaigns wasn't a good leader for the nation. Politicans that made laws for them to have a better life at the expense of the people, and fail to provide the people with liberty, justice, and feedom later became a victim of treachery. Police officers are to protect the people and serve the criminal with their due cause of their criminal lifestyle, but they are using their authority to undermine the innocent with the same brutality. This art of psychological skullduggery is been implemented by every possible means, whether by books, movies, magazines, the local and world-wide news broadcasting systems, school curriculum of education, medically, foods, the internet, politically, religiously, so-call wars, businesses, drugs(pain-killers), street-drugs and mainly television which all implement psychological and physiological effects. All these mechanisms are forms of propaganda to indoctrinate the masses for control and power. Man can't handle too much power. It has been proven by men and women before our times. Any person that desires control and power over others, at all cost are victims of their own insecurities and self-worth. It's different to control to keep order for the betterment of the whole, but just for a selected few without the right means of doing it is ludicrous. If the masters misuse this art of psychological skullduggery, and it causes destruction for all the people for their means of total control, which means they will have to do away with the same ones that aided and helped them achieve their power and control. I like to extend my gratitude to all sincere people that are working and doing all they can for the betterment of human-kind. I know it's not easy, but it's worth going through and doing that what needs to be done. Psychological skullduggery is a great art, tactic, and strategy for control. Innocent people have been pawns for the puppeteers to implement their plans, which is to create room to utilize the art of the plan. Internal strifes and great catastrophes are the way to distract the people and carry out schemes and plans for unlimited power and control. This has been done in history for over thousands of years by rulers, dictators, monarchs, and tyrants that desired power. Man fail to understand that there's a plan and perfect order that is more powerful than what he can ever put into effect. This great Universal Order is what gave birth to man and this universe we call home. This Great Order will take back man's energy and will for life faster when man wrongly uses his abilities. The worst enemy that any person can have is a enemy that has nothing to loose and nothing to gain. The enemy that knows that war will always have its casualties and deaths, and still remain determined to fight is the worst enemy anybody could ask for or have. The enemy that is willing to die yet still determined to fight is the best solider and enemy on the field of battle.

My intention was not to belittle anyone whether leader or would-be leader. My soul desire was to enrich todays leaders with more insight on the power of skullduggery that's slipping through their hands no matter how firm they try to hold their power and control. Politicians and the public are forever caught in a paradox of rights and wrongs, justice and injustice, and mainly hopes and despairs. Religious leaders have failed to be honest, dignified and have the spirit of being a great administrative spiritual leader for the lowly people in need. Todays religious leaders have no respect by the people mainly because the people are witnessing their spiritual leaders' corruption, and can't get the help and aide of some sort. No matter how ambitious, bold and ruthless the leaders are, the have-nots are just as bold to have. The haves are the oppresors that oppresses the have-nots, because of the oppressors greed to have more, which takes away from the have-nots who are trying to live on a meager salary that creates a great dividing line. So, death has a way of evening the score between the haves and the have-nots. Death liberates the have-nots from poverty and daily struggles to survive in societal elite prejudicial discretion system. Death also comes to do justice to the ones that implement injustice, to liberate the have-nots from the haves that take through greed and unjust means. This art of psychological skullduggery has been misused greatly, but it has rewarded those that utilized her with great audacity, clarity and prudence. I know this from experience, and there's much more that could be said about psychological skullduggery. I will not at this time go into further details on the depths and the inner core of this art of psychology, because many wouldn't understand this great art which I have expounded on with clarity. I will leave the rest under that great Hermetic Seal until futher due.

*Remember that influences, propaganda and indoctrinations are forms of psychological skullduggery.^

So, I will just continue to have my little enjoyments that come from my three jewels(my kids), meditation of solitude, ritualizing and economically building with the B.Y.E. Brotherhood and the Ausarian Order, drinking my Chianti red wine, smoking my Carlos Torano cigars, and enjoying myself while sitting in the godly breeze with a book of ancient times. In the midst of reading, I've many times contemplated on life mysteries and greatness. It's really shocking to see so many that misunderstand this great Order and how all things are fashioned so greatly and why many fail to see it. I also, read deeply to understand men and women of olden days that understood liberty, justice, and freedom for all and endure to bring it to fruition and sustain it for the future of the people. Sovereignty is slipping through human hand's every moment without them realizing it, because man is too wrapped up into his or her unlimited egos, illusions, and abstract ambitions. So, this struggle for equilibruim is an ongoing process for man. Mankind can't continue on this road, which will only cause mores strifes, conflicts, and more deaths before he wakes up to his own misused devices. Until then I pray that God intervenes on our behalf for all humanities sake, because man can't see or feel the great magnificent vibrations of life flowing through his veins here and now.

Thanks, Praises, Honor, and Gratitude to, Amen Ra, and the god-mother Linda and god-father John, Sr.

Sincerely,
P.Los

"Words of Warning"

Do not lend this book to anyone, which contains the way of obtaining and keeping power and control, that's been used from ancient times to the present!

"Do not teach or show the pawns or suckers of today how to be Kings, Queens, Prince, Princess, Rulers, and Leaders, which this book provides the art form and way of obtaining that crown of glory!"

"I'm going to end this with a little humor and realness' with all sincerity, and I want you think about this. Check this out, "<u>Life at this present time is more funky than the gas you blow out your ass!</u>" Think about that!!

SELECTED BOOKS FOR READING

Niccolo Machiavelli, The Prince first published in 1513/ Translation copyright © 1966 Bantam Books/ First published by Bantam Books in1966 Translated, Edited and Introduction by Daniel Donno

Niccolo Machiavelli, The Discourses/ Published by Penguin Books in 1970 /Edited with an Introduction copyright © 1970 by Bernard Crick/ Using The Translation of Leslie J. Walker, S.J./ with Revisions by Brian Richardson

Nine Lives By Plutarch, Makers of Rome/ First Published by Penguin Books in 1965/ Copyright © Ian Scott-Kilvert, 1965 Translated with an Introduction by Ian Scott-Kilvert

Cicero, Political Speeches/ © D. H. Berry 2006 First Published as an Oxford World's Classics paperback 2006/ Translated with Introductions and Notes by D.H. Berry

Cicero, The Republic And The Laws/First Published as an Oxford World Classic paperback 1998/ Translation © by Niall Rudd 1998 and Editorial Matter © by Jonathan Powell and Niall Rudd 1998

Sun Tzu, The Art Of War/ © Oxford University Press, 1963 First Published by The Clarendon Press, 1963 First Issued as an Oxfors University Press Paperback, 1971 Translated and with an Introduction by Samuel Griffith/with a foreword by B.H. Liddell Hart

Cicero, The Good Life/ Published by the Penguin Group, Pengiun Books Ltd, Registered Offices : Harmondsworth, Middlesex, England / First Published 1971 Translation, Introductio an Notes copyright Michael Grant Publication Ltd, 1971 Printed in England by Clays Ltd, 1971 St Ives plc Set in Monotype Bembo

Jean-Jacques Rousseau, The Social Contact/Penguin Books Ltd, Registered Offices: Harmondsworth, Middlesex/ This translation first published 1968 Copyright © Maurice Cranston, 1968

Marion Johson, The Borgias/Penguin Books/ First Published by Macdonald 1981/Published as a

Paul Strathern, Machiavelli In 90 Minutes/ Copyright © 1998 by Paul Strathern

Robert Greene, The Concise Art of Seduction/ Derived from *The Art of Seduction,* which was first published in Great Britian 2001 by Profile Books and first published in the United States by Viking Penguin, a member of Penguin Putnam Inc./ Copyright © Robert Greene and Joost Elffers, 2001, 2003

Mickey Royal, Pimp Game: An Instructional Manual/ Copyright ©1998 by Mikail Sharif

John H. Davis, Mafia Dynasty: *The Rise and Fall of the Gambino Crime Family/* Copyright © 1993 by John H. Davis/ HarperCollins Publishers, Inc.

George Wolf with Joseph Dimona, Frank Costello: *Prime Minister of the Underworld/* A Bantam Book / published by arrangement with William Morrow & Company, Inc./ Morrow edition published June 1974/ Bantam edition / June 1975 / Copyright © 1974 by George Wolf and Joseph Dimona

Deborrah Himsel, Leadership Sopranos *Style*: How To Become a More Effective Boss/ © 2004 by Deborah Himself / Published by Dearborn Trade Publishing

Abram N. Shulsky, Silent Warfare: *Understanding The World Of intelligence,* second edition, revised / revised by Gary J. Schmitt/ Foreword by Roy Godson/ Copyright © 1993 by Brassey's

Derek Wilson © Copyright 1988, Rothschild: A Story Of Wealth and Power/by Mandarin Paperbacks

Thom Burnett and Alex Games: Who Really Runs The World?/ © 2007 Conspiracy Books Published by The Disinformation Company Ltd. 163 Third avenue, Suite 108 New York, NY 10003

Alistair McAlpine Copyright ©1998 all rights reserved/ The New Machiavelli: the art of politics in business/ Published by John Wiley & Sons, Inc.

William Davis, Text copyright © 2006: The Rich/ Published in the UK in 2006 by Icon Books Ltd, The Old Dairy, Brook Road, Thriplow, Cambridge SG8 7RG

Robert Lacey, Copyright © 1991; Little Man: Meyer Lansky and The Gangster Life/ Published by Little, Brown and Company

Alan Axelrod, Copyright © 2003/ Nothing To Fear: Lessons in Leadership from FDR

Adolf Hitler; Mein Kampf/Translated By Ralph Manheim Copyright © Renewed 1971 by The Houghton Mifflin Company

Midas Jones/ The Modern Prince: *Better Living Through Machiavellianism*/ Copyright © 2088 by Midas Jones

L. F. Gunlicks/ The *Machiavellian* Manager's Handbook For Success/ Copyright © 1993 by Lynn F. Gunlicks

Paul Babiak, Ph. D. and Robert D. Hare, Ph. D./ Snakes in Suits: *When Psychopaths go To work*/ Copyright © 2006

Iceberg Slim/ The Naked Soul of Iceberg Slim: *Robert Beck's Real Story*/ Copyright © 1971, 1986 by Holloway House Publishing Company

Playa-i$m: Are you a player
or Are you being played?